Ian Rankin's

Black & Blue

Christopher Nicol

Association for Scottish Literary Studies 2008

Published by
Association for Scottish Literary Studies
Department of Scottish Literature
7 University Gardens
University of Glasgow
Glasgow G12 8QH
www.asls.org.uk

ASLS is a registered charity no. SC006535

First published 2008

A CIP catalogue for this title is available from the British
Library

ISBN 978-0-948877-90-2

The Association for Scottish Literary Studies
acknowledges the support of the Scottish Arts Council
towards the publication of this book

Typeset by AFS Image Setters Ltd, Glasgow
Printed by Bell & Bain Ltd, Glasgow

CONTENTS

	Page
Ian Rankin and his work	1
Black & Blue: the social landscape	7
John Rebus in *Black & Blue*	14
Rebus's empathy with victims and underdogs	16
Rebus's lack of respect for establishment figures	19
Rebus and personal engagement	25
Characters	32
Detective Inspector Jack Morton	32
Detective Sergeant Ludovic Lumsden	34
Chief Inspector Charles Ancram	37
Bible John	39
Detective Sergeant Brian Holmes	43
Themes	46
The power of past sins	46
Fathers and children	49
The effects of the oil industry	52
Structure and style	57
Bibliography	62

All page references are to the text published in the Orion paperback edition.

SCOTNOTES

Study guides to major Scottish writers and literary texts

Produced by the Education Committee
of the Association for Scottish Literary Studies

THE ASSOCIATION FOR SCOTTISH LITERARY STUDIES aims to promote the study, teaching and writing of Scottish literature, and to further the study of the languages of Scotland.

To these ends, the ASLS publishes works of Scottish literature; literary criticism and in-depth reviews of Scottish books in *Scottish Studies Review*; short articles, features and news in *ScotLit*; and scholarly studies of language in *Scottish Language*. It also publishes *New Writing Scotland*, an annual anthology of new poetry, drama and short fiction, in Scots, English and Gaelic. ASLS has also prepared a range of teaching materials covering Scottish language and literature for use in schools.

All the above publications are available as a single "package", in return for an annual subscription. Enquiries should be sent to:

ASLS, Department of Scottish Literature, 7 University Gardens, University of Glasgow, Glasgow G12 8QH. Telephone/fax +44 (0)141 330 5309, e-mail **office@asls.org.uk** or visit our website at **www.asls.org.uk**

EDITORS' FOREWORD

The *Scotnotes* booklets are a series of study guides to major Scottish writers and literary texts that are likely to be elements within literature courses. They are aimed at senior pupils in secondary schools and students in further education colleges and colleges of education. Each booklet in the series is written by a person who is not only an authority on the particular writer or text but also experienced in teaching at the relevant levels in schools or colleges. Furthermore, the editorial board, composed of members of the Education Committee of the Association for Scottish Literary Studies, considers the suitability of each booklet for the students in question.

For many years there has been a shortage of readily accessible critical notes for the general student of Scottish literature. *Scotnotes* has grown as a series to meet this need, and provides students with valuable aids to the understanding and appreciation of the key writers and major texts within the Scottish literary tradition.

Lorna Borrowman Smith
Ronald Renton

IAN RANKIN AND HIS WORK

Ian Rankin was born on the 28th April 1960 in the Fife mining village of Cardenden, a birthplace shared with his most famous fictional creation, John Rebus. His father, James, worked as a grocer in Lochgelly before transferring to office work at the naval dockyard in Rosyth, dying in 1990. His mother, Isobel, was originally from Yorkshire and died when Ian was eighteen.

From an early age Rankin used the environment of Cardenden as a creative stimulus, seeking to transcend its limitations by conjuring up alternative worlds:

> We used to call it 'Car-dead-end', if that gives you the picture. But the place did kind of prime me for writing because in the 1960s, when the Scottish coal mines all closed out for economic reasons, and even as a 6-year-old you could see the hope seeping out of the town, I found escape through my imagination. I tried to create a better world in my mind, a world in which Cardenden was a kind of exciting place to be. I was always an obsessive sort of kid, and I just took my imagination to extremes, you know. I used to write stories and make up comic books and stuff like that, anything to vent my imagination.
>
> It wasn't enough just to read comic books, I had to make up my own, complete with stick men and speech bubbles. I made up a pop group called Kaput, after the lead singer, Ian Kaput, and in the comics I created a whole world around them, an alternative universe where they were always number one and they went on tour. And I even wrote song lyrics for them.
>
> (Interview with J. Kingston Pierce januarymagazine.com/profiles/ianrankin.html)

Educated at Denend Primary School, Auchterderran Junior High School and at Beath High School in Cowdenbeath, Rankin later read English Language and Literature at Edinburgh University where specialised in American literature, graduating in 1982.

This specialisation in American literature was hardly surprising given that while haunting the local library as a youngster he had come under the influence of works such as *The Godfather, One Flew Over the Cuckoo's Nest* and, perhaps more significantly for anyone studying the Rebus novels, the *Shaft* series of books written by Ernest Tidyman about a black private detective in New York whose central character, John Shaft, shares more than a first name with Rebus, both being loners with uncompromising attitudes to life and authority.

In his first year at Edinburgh University he joined a short-lived New Wave band called *The Dancing Pigs*, which was a name he used again for the favourite pop group of Allan Mitchison, the murdered oil worker, in *Black & Blue*. This brief involvement was enough to convince Rankin that the life of a professional musician would never be his, although music was to remain a passion, as the frequent references to groups and singers throughout the Rebus series readily testify. Indeed, amongst his first literary efforts had been song lyrics for Kaput, his own fictional pop group. This had led on to poetry writing, for which he won a school prize and later had a poem published while still at school. Although he continued to write poetry prolifically at university, despatching poems to publications such as *The Listener, Literary Review*, and *The Times Literary Supplement*, he did not repeat the successes of his school-days. He was more successful, however, with his short story endeavours, coming runner-up to Iain Crichton Smith in a short story competition run by *The Scotsman* newspaper and winning another short story contest organized by *Radio Forth*.

Although his first love was American literature, he embarked on a PhD on the works of Muriel Spark in 1983. This he never completed, using the funding largely to write three novels instead. The first of these, *Summer Rites*, has never been published. The second was *The Flood* which came out in 1986. The third was *Knots and Crosses* in which Rebus made his first appearance. It was published by Polygon in 1987 after five other publishing houses had turned it down. In the tradition of R. L. Stevenson's *Dr Jekyll and Mr Hyde* and James Hogg's *Confessions of a Justified Sinner*, *Knots and Crosses* takes up the idea of the split personality popularised in the earlier classics. *Knots and Crosses* has at its heart a serial killer who is also a children's librarian. This duality in peoples' lives was an idea that Rankin was to return to in later novels, notably in *Black & Blue* where figures such as Ludovic Lumsden, Major Weir and Ryan Slocum all lead somewhat Jekyll and Hyde existences. Indeed, the oil industry around which the novel revolves is itself something of a Jekyll and Hyde entity in Rankin's handling of it, evincing as it does an outward legitimacy and prosperity, yet harbouring darker elements which are not immediately obvious.

The year 1986 was a significant one for Rankin. As well having *The Flood* published, he married Miranda Harvey (who had been a year ahead of him at university) and moved to London. At this time Miranda was a civil servant, running the private office of Francis Maude, Minister for Trade in the Thatcher government of the period. Rankin found work at the National Folktale Centre before becoming an editorial assistant at *Hi-Fi Review* and later its editor.

Meanwhile he continued to write and was elected a Hawthornden Fellow in 1988 and won the 1991 Chandler-Fulbright Award for detective fiction. This prestigious award brought with it a cash prize which could only be spent in America, resulting in Rankin and his wife touring the States for six months in 1992.

The London years saw the emergence of *Watchman* (1988) and *Westwind* (1990), and the next Rebus novel, *Hide and Seek* (1990). In 1990, leaving the stress and pressure of London behind them, the couple moved to the Dordogne region of France where they believed they could live more cheaply and Rankin could devote himself full-time to writing.

The move was not an unmitigated success. While the French years saw the appearance of four Rebus novels, a book of Rebus short stories and three thrillers under the

pseudonym Jack Harvey (Jack being the name of his first
son and Harvey the maiden name of his wife), Rankin
missed Scotland, money was still a problem and by living
abroad Rankin was not readily available for the
promotional circuit beloved of publishers. Much more
critically, it became obvious early in 1995 that the younger
of their two sons born in France, Kit, was seriously
handicapped. He was diagnosed as suffering from Angelman's
Syndrome, a severe developmental disorder. Living as the
Rankins did in the depths of rural France, far from
specialist help, the months which followed were difficult
ones. These were the months which also saw the genesis of
Black & Blue and much of Rankin's pain went into its
writing. Interviewed by Danuta Kean for *The Independent*
22 October 2006 Rankin relates that:

> I would go home from hospital every day and
> try and write this book. I really put Rebus
> through the wringer emotionally. There is one
> scene where he has a fight with his best friend
> ... and he is down on his knees, with snot
> coming out of his nose, crying, full of rage,
> fear and frustration. That was me, not
> physically, but emotionally.

The upshot was that the couple moved back to Edinburgh in 1996 and in 1997 *Black & Blue* appeared, winning
that same year the much-coveted Crime Writers' Association Macallan Gold Dagger for Fiction. The pain and
anger that had gone into its creation had helped produce a
much denser and more socially probing work than any of
the others in the Rebus canon to date. According to
Rankin's editor, Caroline Oakley, interviewed by Nicholas
Wroe for *Guardian Unlimited Books* 28 May 2005, *Black &
Blue* marked a commercial breakthrough:

> Ian had written eight or nine books by then,
> which were selling about 30,000 in paperback,
> which is okay, but people at the publisher
> were asking how long can we put money
> behind him. We needed one more big effort
> and he pulled it off.

After the success of *Black & Blue*, sales soared and Rankin can now, according to his editor, count on selling half a million copies in paperback within three months of publication. He has been awarded honorary doctorates from the universities of Abertay, St Andrews, Edinburgh, Hull and from the Open University. He was made an OBE in 2002 for services to literature.

Black & Blue marked more than a commercial break-through, however, for many of the novels which followed manifested not only a newly found density and complexity of plotlines but a keener awareness of contemporary social issues. Admittedly, this had been present before in Rankin's output, as for example, in *Mortal Causes* (1994) where sectarianism and paramilitary activities were important elements in the plot but in *Black & Blue* the moral and social issues connected with the decommissioning of North Sea oil platforms and the influence of the industry in general may be seen to be becoming more all-embracing of the novel's life. A sharp alertness to contemporary issues allied to deftly skilful layering of multiple plot lines now became a feature of the novels which followed.

The Hanging Garden (1998) looked at the criminal fallout from the Bosnian and Chechen conflict on Edinburgh as well as the enigma of a supposedly rehabilitated Nazi war criminal. *Dead Souls* (1999) examined the issue of the treatment of convicted paedophiles while *Set in Darkness* (2000) explored issues surrounding Scottish devolution. *The Falls* (2001) and *A Question of Blood* (2003) both dealt with the corrosive influence of the internet. *Resurrection Men* (2002) raised the issue of police corruption. In *Fleshmarket Close* (2004) Rankin has Rebus involving himself with the question of people trafficking while *The Naming of the Dead* (2006) has as its backdrop arms sales and the G8 meeting on global poverty at Gleneagles in 2005.

Rankin explained this concern with social issues in an interview with *The Bookseller* 9 February 2001:

> [...] crime fiction deals with contemporary issues in a way that the literary novel is refusing to do. If you look at the Booker and

Whitbread shortlists, there's an awful lot of
looking back, and not much about what's
becoming of us in this new Internet age, this
corporate age, this leisure industry age. Crime
novels and thrillers are the ones dealing with
that.

This is a view of crime fiction in general and of Rankin
in particular shared by novelist and critic Allan Massie,
interviewed by Nicholas Wroe for *Guardian Unlimited
Books* 28 May 2005:

One of the advantages of the crime novel is
that it deals more convincingly with different
levels of society than is now easy to do in a
straight novel. Ian writes very seriously about
modern society.

The paradox highlighted by both men is that the crime
fiction genre is treating mainstream issues in a way which,
in their view, mainstream fiction no longer seems to be
doing. Rankin's triumph is that his treatment of the important issues of the day provokes thought yet at the same
time entertains grippingly thanks to its mix of vividly
original characters, incisive dialogue and intricately
layered plots which keep the reader working hard to keep
up with its multiple strands and twists.

BLACK & BLUE: THE SOCIAL LANDSCAPE

When *Black & Blue* was published in 1997 it was the eighth Rankin novel to feature his character Inspector John Rebus. In six of these previous books, Rebus had been largely confined by his creator to probing the criminal underbelly of Edinburgh. (The other, *Tooth and Nail*, sees him investigating in London.)

In *Black & Blue* Rankin tackles a much broader canvas. As well as revisiting familiar Edinburgh haunts and characters, Rebus investigates not only in Glasgow, Aberdeen and the Shetlands but is carried still further afield to visit a soon-to-be-decommissioned North Sea oil platform and even a surviving two-thousand-year-old broch on the island of Mousa.

Similarly disparate are the plotlines that Rankin sets Rebus to deal with. These include the death of a North Sea oil worker in Edinburgh and the investigation into a serial killer who has struck in Edinburgh, Glasgow and Aberdeen, one who models his killings on the murders of a real-life 1960s murderer – Bible John. One of Rankin's real achievements here is to have this real-life character turn up in the pages of fiction to deal with the 'upstart' who is bringing unwanted and threatening attention to his past crimes and present identity. Adding to this complex mix of storylines is a television (and later police) investigation into a possible miscarriage of justice in which Rebus may have been complicit two decades previously. A further complication is the serious, personal crisis that Rebus undergoes in the midst of dealing with his professional concerns. Adding still more to Rebus's concerns is the fate of the marriage of his colleague and protégé, Brian Holmes. Unsurprisingly, given the breadth of this canvas, the resulting text was the longest of the Rebus series at that time, running to almost five hundred pages.

Written while he was living in south-west France, Rankin uses his distance to focus much more broadly on Scotland than in previous Rebus novels. *Black & Blue* has, therefore, a real claim to be seen as a 'state-of-the-nation' novel.

How then does Rebus see Scotland in the closing days of the twentieth century?

The answer is partly suggested by the novel's title: *Black & Blue*, taken from an album by the Rolling Stones. The 'black' at one level is a reference to the black of North Sea oil, the industry which forms, not only a backdrop to the machinations of the plot, but which triggers many of them as well. At another, black and blue are colours symptomatic of the malaise that seems to lie over the Scotland depicted here, in that the outlook at many levels throughout the novel – personal, social and cultural – is bleak not to say black and Scotland seems to be suffering from its own form of 'the blues'. *Black & Blue* is a novel which unfolds against the background of an industry nearing the end of its natural life, the problems inherent in wrapping it up and the allied crime and corruption that its wealth has attracted over the years.

As Rebus drives into Aberdeen, he reflects on its look of 'impermanence' and comments wryly on Scotland's rulers' habitual lack of planning and foresight:

> For all the associations with granite, Aberdeen had a feeling of impermanence. These days it owed almost everything it had to oil, and the oil wouldn't be there for ever. Growing up in Fife, Rebus had seen the same thing with coal: no one planned for the day it would run out. When it did, hope ran out with it.
> Linwood, Bathgate, the Clyde: nobody ever seemed to learn. (p163)

These latter references to the failed industries of coal mining, car manufacture and ship building help broaden the novel's resonance well beyond the parameters of the crimes under investigation here.

But the malaise covers more than just the failures, past or present, of Scotland's industries and planners. Rankin, here, as in later Rebus novels, is a sharp commentator on the broader social fallout for which these failures in macroeconomic matters are, to an extent, responsible. What he sees around Rebus's daily life is grim. In his office in

Craigmillar, far from the direct influence of the oil industry, Rebus reflects on the social deprivation to be observed in many of the housing estates around Edinburgh, the result – ironically in this instance – of too *much* not too *little* planning:

> Niddrie, Craigmillar, Wester Hailes, Muirhouse, Pilton, Granton ... They all seemed to him like some horrible experiment in social engineering: scientists in white coats sticking families down in this maze or that, seeing what would happen, how strong they'd have to become to cope, whether or not they'd find the exit ... (p106)

The reality he sees around 'Fort Apache', the local nickname for the Craigmillar police station, is squalid and redolent of crime and social inequalities:

> The shops in front of Fort Apache were the usual metal shutters and mesh grille affairs, Asian owners mostly, even if the shops were staffed with white faces. Men hung around the on the street outside, T-shirted, sporting tattoos, smoking. Eyes as trustworthy as a weasel in a hen-house.
>
> Eggs? Not me, pal, can't stand them.
>
> Rebus bought cigarettes and a newspaper. Walking out of the shop, a baby buggy caught his ankles, a woman told him to mind where he was fucking going. She bustled away, hauling a toddler behind her. Twenty, maybe twenty-one, hair dyed blonde, two front teeth missing. Her bared forearms showed tattoos, too. Across the road, an advertising hoarding told him to spend £20k on a new car. (p55)

Rebus returns to these inequalities again while waiting with Jack Morton for a meeting with a journalist elsewhere in Edinburgh:

> They waited for her in the lounge. Jack flicked through *Scottish Field* and kept reading out descriptions of estates for sale: 'seven

thousand acres in Caithness, with hunting
lodge, stabling, and working farm'. He looked
up at Rebus.

'Some country this, eh? Where else could
you lay your hands on seven thousand acres
at knockdown prices?'

'There's a theatre group called 7:84 – know
what it means?'

'What?'

'Seven per cent of the population controls
eighty-four per cent of the wealth.'

'Are we in the seven?'

Rebus snorted. 'Not even close, Jack.' (p348)

Scenes of social deprivation are not confined to Edinburgh. Visiting 'Uncle Joe' Toal, in his Glasgow housing
estate, Rebus observes a community equally deprived:

The housing scheme, when they reached it,
was much like any scheme its size in Edinburgh: grey pebbledash, barren play areas,
tarmac and a smattering of fortified shops.
Kids on bikes stopping to watch the car, eyes
as keen as sentries'; brisk baby buggies,
shapeless mothers with dyed blonde hair.
Further into the estate, driving slowly: people
watching from behind their windows, men
at pavement corners, muttered confabs. A
city within a city, uniform and enervating,
energy sapped, nothing left but obstinacy [...]
(p89)

Even in the pockets of prosperity created by the oil
industry – and Rankin does not overlook the real prosperity
brought in its wake to Shetland and the North-East – there
is a depressing lack of real identity and social cohesion.
When Rebus goes to visit Jake Harley's partner at their
home at Brae in Shetland he notices that:

Brae looked to be suffering a crisis of identity,
like it had suddenly plopped into being and
didn't know what to make of itself. The houses
were new but anonymous; there was obviously
money around, but it couldn't buy everything.

> It couldn't turn Brae back into the village it
> had been in the days before Sullom Voe.
> (p217)

Interestingly, even the serial killer, Bible John, identifies
(in a location very different from Brae) this same crisis of
identity. Commenting on Glasgow he says:

> In the late sixties, it had been reinventing
> itself: knocking down old slums, building their
> concrete equivalents on the outskirts. New
> roads, bridges, motorways – the place had
> been an enormous building site. He got the
> feeling the process was still ongoing, as if the
> city still hadn't acquired an identity it could
> be comfortable with. (p57)

It can be argued, of course, that a policeman by the very
nature of his job investigating crime will perhaps see a
grimmer side of people and places than most of us. Does not
such a perspective give an unbalanced view of reality? This
is an argument of which Ian Rankin is himself very much
aware. In *Rebus's Scotland* (2005: 128) he comments:

> I'm conscious of a question readers may well
> want answering: can crime fiction ever give a
> true and all-embracing account of a nation?
> The answer should be a resounding 'Yes!', but
> only if we include works by the likes of
> Dickens and Dostoevsky under the umbrella
> term of 'crime'.

By this Rankin appears to imply that, in works by these
authors, crime takes place against a wider social, cultural
and economic background which may well be as significant
and as of much interest as the crimes themselves and which
may, if not excuse, at least explain the reasons for these
crimes. Furthermore, the fact remains that, while only a
small number of the people affected by the social conditions
described earlier will actually become victims of crime or
commit crimes, countless others will continue to live out
their existence in these bleak, soulless conditions. These
folk, as much as do criminals themselves, people the pages
of Rankin's novels and create the rich, social tapestry that

helps explain in part some of the popularity of the Rebus novels.

In looking into events in such social conditions Rankin appears to consider that he and Rebus share a common purpose:

> [...] it seems to me that the figures of the detective and the novelist are similar in some ways. Both seek the truth, through creating a narrative from apparently chaotic or unconnected events. Both are interested in human nature and motivation. (pp30–1)

In the same study Rankin later returns to and develops this idea (p129):

> What crime writers can do is explore why crimes occur, what effect they have, and what they tell us about the world we've chosen to create for ourselves.

Rebus, while inspecting the murder site of Johnny Bible's fourth victim, goes even further:

> 'There's a question I've been asking myself. Do we let it happen, or do we make it happen? (p276)

Rebus's query hovers over much of *Black & Blue*. Is society the victim of criminality or its creator? This is a question which the frequent references to the many ills of contemporary Scottish society amply foreground. If the kind of world we see at work and play in *Black & Blue* is the one we've chosen to create for ourselves, what does this say about us?

By the novel's close we have certainly been made aware of the identity of the perpetrators of various crimes, for this, after all, is ostensibly a 'whodunit'. Strangely, however, the identity of the perpetrators – the gist of much crime fiction – is not what remains with us once we have closed the novel. We learn that Johnny Bible, whose tracking down has accounted for much of the novel's focus, is one Martin Davidson but the discovery of his identity – and dead body – is almost an anticlimax. (Nor can police investigations take any credit for ridding society of his menace.) Allan Mitchison's death, which took Rebus to Aberdeen in the first place, may or may not have been intentional. Even the apprehension of criminals whom the law in the end appears to be bringing to book – Malky Toal, Judd Fuller, Ludovic Lumsden, D. I. Jenkins and Uncle Joe Toal – brings us no great satisfaction.

The goal of much traditional crime fiction – the unmasking of the guilty – is not what appears to interest Rankin principally here. At the end of a work of traditional crime fiction, the guilty are exposed, the guiltless exonerated and society at large returned to normality, cleansed of the offending characters. But in *Black & Blue* no such return to normality seems possible. For what kind of 'normality' is it when T-Bird Oil may still manage to dump its abandoned oil platforms in the North Sea, when an incestuous abuser of his daughter continues to retain a respected place in the business community, when a question mark continues to hang over the honesty of the police force of at least one major Scottish city, when the homeless such as Mick Hine and old Frank sit around on park benches and disappear in the winter 'like migrating bird[s]' ... Or if this *is* the normality to which we are being returned, then we share Rebus's pain and guilt as he surveys it and come closer to understanding his frequent rage and frustration at 'the world we've chosen to create for ourselves', in Rankin's own phrase.

In the pages of *Black & Blue* we encounter much more than crimes and criminals. We are introduced to themes, characters and situations which give us not only a panoramic glimpse of in Scotland in the closing days of the 20th century, but also an insight into a world whose underlying social and moral ills may be all too familiar and painful to observers of contemporary society well beyond Scotland's borders.

JOHN REBUS IN *BLACK & BLUE*

Towering over the complex action of *Black & Blue* is the
equally complex character of Detective Inspector John
Rebus. He is a tormented human being yet an ultimately
effective detective, one whose unorthodox methods, however, break many of the rules of police procedure and which
expose him both to professional censure and personal
danger. As well as involving him in these latter two
hazards, however, (a situation after all not unknown to
crime-fiction detectives), *Black & Blue*, is a novel which
sees Rebus having to face up to a personal crisis un-
precedented in his life to date.

Earlier, we have seen how the term 'black and blue'
refers in part to the malaise that seems to lie over Scotland
in the closing years of the 20[th]century. It is a term which
applies equally well to the character of John Rebus himself
as depicted here. In the previous novels in which he
appears, John Rebus is no stranger to the 'blues', locked as
he is in the solitary world of the divorced, hard-drinking
detective. Here, however, his 'blues' take on a darker
dimension as Rebus plunges deeper into a nervous/
emotional crisis more profound than any encountered so
far. It is one brought on partly by a bad conscience over the
re-emergence of miscarriage of justice he may have helped
bring about decades previously and partly by abuse of
his own health by heavy drinking and disregard for his
personal welfare over many years. As the tempo of the
various cases he is juggling accelerates and the frustrations
and pressure on him mount, he suffers an explosion of rage
and self-loathing which results in a cathartic fistfight with
his old friend, Jack Morton.

> Teeth bared, Jack swung again, even more
> wildly, giving his friend plenty of time to
> dodge and launch a punch of his own. Rebus
> almost defended himself, but thought better of
> it. Instead he waited for the impact. Jack hit
> him low, the sort of blow that could wind a
> man without doing damage. Rebus doubled
> over, fell to hands and knees, and spewed on

> to the ground, spitting out mostly liquid. He
> went on trying to cough everything out, even
> when there was nothing left to expel. And
> then he started crying. Crying for himself and
> for Lawson Geddes, and maybe even for Lenny
> Spaven. And most of all for Elsie Rhind and
> all her sisters, all the victims he couldn't help
> and would never be able to help.
>   [...] The crying seemed to take forever. Then
> he felt the shuddering lessen, stop altogether
> [...]
>   'Christ,' he said I needed that.'
>   'I haven't had a fight like that since I was
> a teenager,' Jack said. 'Feel better?'
>   'Much.' (p325)

To understand how Rebus arrives at this point and why
he undergoes this crisis we need to look more closely at the
personality of the man himself, for not every detective faced
with similar problems would have reacted in this dramatic,
soul-baring way. Who exactly is John Rebus?

One appraisal of him is given by Bible John after he
has searched Rebus's flat in an attempt to retrieve the
business card which he had foolishly given to him, not
knowing he was a policeman:

> He felt now he *knew* Rebus, at least to a
> degree – he felt the loneliness of his life, the
> gaps where sentiment and warmth and love
> should have been. There was music, and there
> were books, but neither in great quantity nor
> of great quality. The clothes were utilitarian,
> one jacket much like another. No shoes. He
> found that bizarre in the extreme. Did the
> man possess only one pair? (p361)

To an extent, Bible John is correct. To the world, Rebus
presents a poor picture. A bouncer at Burke's Club sizes
him up and

> Rebus knew what he saw: a middle-aged lush,
> a pathetic figure in a cheap suit. (p225)

But the personality and interior life of the man cannot

be so easily dismissed and the reader – like the Burke's
Club bouncer – is soon disabused. So what lies behind the
somewhat grubby exterior?

Rebus's empathy with victims and underdogs
Describing Rebus's character in *Rebus's Scotland*, Ian Rankin
comments:

> Rebus is affected by every case he works on,
> and carries with him the ghosts of every victim.
> (p20)

It is perhaps this sensibility to the suffering of victims
that makes Rebus the attractive figure he is to readers, his
other faults notwithstanding.

Throughout *Black & Blue* we see very clearly how cases
past and present affect him personally. 'Else Rhind and all
her sisters' were not the only murder victims to haunt him.
He became involved emotionally in the Johnny Bible case
because he knew and liked the killer's second victim, Angie
Riddell, an Edinburgh prostitute. Mulling over how dead
victims may haunt those charged with the investigation of
their murders he remarks:

> [...] sometimes if you listened hard enough
> you could hear them screaming. Sitting in his
> chair by the window, Rebus had heard many a
> despairing cry. One night, he'd heard Angie
> Riddell and it had pierced his heart, because
> he had known her, liked her. In that instant it
> had become personal for him. (p51)

Unlike some fellow officers, he insists always on the
victim's dignity. When a colleague refers crudely to Allan
Mitchison, an oil worker killed by being impaled on a
railing, Rebus's reaction is an implied rebuke:

> 'I get the feeling Spike maybe worked for an
> oil company.'
> 'His name was Allan Mitchison,' Rebus
> replied quietly. (p24)

His empathy with Mitchison is seen again later. Through
an acknowledgement to Mitchison in a cheaply produced

Xeroxed concert programme, Rebus discovers that Mitchison had been engaged in organising a Dancing Pigs' concert to raise money for environmental protests:

> Allan Mitchison had played his part organising the gig, and here was his reward – and memorial.
> 'I'll see if I can do better,' Rebus said, rolling the programme into his pocket. (p259)

Even in moments of personal stress (under investigation – ludicrous though it is – as a suspect in the killing of Johnny Bible's fourth victim) he asks to view the scene of the murder, to the puzzlement of an uncomprehending superior, unaffected in any way by the death of the girl:

> 'Do me one favour,' Rebus said.
> 'What?' They were back in the back of Ancram's car, heading for Rebus's hotel, where they'd picked up his car.
> 'A quick detour down to the docks.'
> Ancram glanced at him. 'Why?'
> 'I want to see where she died.'
> Ancram looked at him again. 'What for?'
> Rebus shrugged. 'To pay my respects,' he said.
> [...] 'Listen, Rebus ... all this interest is because you once bought a prostitute a cup of tea?'
> 'Her name was Angie Riddell.' Rebus paused. 'She had beautiful eyes.' (p276)

This idea of paying his respects surfaces elsewhere. Walking the route which he speculates Johnny Bible's first victim might have taken with her murderer, he comments:

> It might not be the same route *she* took, and he doubted it would throw up anything like a clue, but he wanted to do it, same as he'd driven down to Leith to pay his respects to Angie Riddell's patch. (pp257–8)

Even in the triumphant moment when he and Siobhan Clarke work out (far ahead of any police force in Scotland) that Johnny Bible must be one Martin Davidson of

LancerTech, an oil industry service company, his immediate
thoughts are not for himself and the success of his own line
of enquiry but for the final peace of Angie Riddell, the
victim he knew:

> Rebus saw her picture again: Angie. Hoped
> she was getting ready to rest. (p462)

Though exposed to multiple murders throughout his
career, Rebus has never allowed the victims to become mere
statistics as they are to some colleagues, insisting not only
on their right to justice but on their humanity and dignity.

His sympathies extend, however, beyond victims of violent
crime: Rebus's is a humanity that in this novel encompasses
underdogs and the marginalized in general. (And in *Black
& Blue* he himself learns at first hand what it is to be a
victim when he is framed and questioned by Ancram and
Grogan as a suspect in the Vanessa Holden inquiry.
Chapter 20)

Present on the Bannock oil platform when Joanna Bruce
and her fellow protestors are brought aboard and handcuff
themselves to the railings, Rebus is far from being at one
with the oil men when they bring up an oxyacetylene torch
cut them loose:

> Rebus had half a mind – maybe more than half
> – to throw the torch over the side.(p256)

Again, seeking out the homeless Mick Hine for information on Lenny Spaven, Rebus reflects perceptively on
another down-and-out he had known. In his repeated phrases
we hear a sad, quiet compassion for Frank and others like
him:

> There used to be one old guy, Frank, Rebus
> saw him every summer, and at the end of
> every summer he disappeared like a migrating
> bird, only to reappear the next year. But this
> year ... this year Frank hadn't appeared. The
> homeless people Rebus saw were a lot younger
> than Frank, his spiritual children, if not grand-
> children; only they were different – tougher
> and more frightened, wired and tired. Different

> game, different rules. Edinburgh's 'gentlemen
> of the road': twenty years ago you could have
> measured them in mere dozens. But not these
> days. Not these days ... (pp321–2)

Comparing himself to Rebus in *Rebus's Scotland*, Ian
Rankin concludes:

> He comes from a slightly older generation
> (albeit the generation which gave the world
> Hendrix and Dylan), and is less liberal than I
> am. (p33)

Taking into account Rebus's empathy with the variety
of victims and outsiders which we have examined here,
Rankin is perhaps being a little harsh on his creation by
seeing him as 'less liberal' than himself, but he is right to
remind us that Rebus is of the generation of Dylan whose
spirit of inclusive humanity towards suffering he unquestionably shares here.

Rebus's lack of respect for establishment figures

Balancing Rebus's sympathy for victims and outsiders is
his feisty disinclination to be overawed by the representatives of big business, the police hierarchy or the media
which he encounters. Part of Rebus's attractiveness to us is
this cocky refusal to be impressed or intimidated by
institutional Scotland. As the novel progresses we applaud
more and more his sarcastic banter and general outspokenness faced with flawed characters such as Major Weir,
Detective Chief Inspectors Ancram and Grogan, Kayleigh
Burgess and Eamon Breen who have all carved out
powerful niches in their different institutions.

This reluctance to be dutifully respectful towards estab-
lishment figures is one of the first features of Rebus's
character which we learn about. It is this trait after all
which has landed him in his present grim posting in
Craigmillar:

> He'd upset some people, people who mattered.
> They hadn't been able to deal him a death
> blow, so had instead consigned him to pur-
> gatory. (p6)

Throughout the novel he will continue to upset 'people who matter' since his loyalty is to a higher authority than theirs. People 'who matter' to Rebus are not the same people 'who matter' to society in general. Rebus, for all his faults, sees justice for society's victims as more important than kowtowing to the powers that be or ingratiating himself into their good graces. Moreover, in Rebus's egalitarian universe, people must earn respect and are not treated to it simply by reason of their office.

We see this at work when pursuing his enquiry into the death of Allan Mitchison. He crosses the path of the President of T-Bird Oil, Major Weir, who is treated with great deference by most people around him. As Rebus and Stuart Minchell, Human Resource manager at T-Bird Oil, go to enter a lift Rebus notices:

> [...] there were already two men inside, which still left room. Minchell hesitated. He looked like he was about to say they'd wait, but Rebus had already stepped inside the lift, so he followed, with a slight bow to one of the men, the elder of the two. (p173)

As the lift reaches ground level, 'Minchell physically held Rebus back until the other two had got out' (p173). Deference of the kind practised by Minchell is unknown to Rebus who maintains an egalitarian disregard for those in privileged positions. He even at times seems to go out of his way to antagonise them with his banter, seemingly irked by the toadying of society at large towards such people. Meeting up with Major Weir again on the plane to Shetland where he is treated with reverential respect by others on the flight, Rebus notes he is 'deep in the *Financial Times*' (p209):

> 'Any chance of a keek at the racing results?'
> [...] 'We met yesterday,' Rebus told him. 'My name's Detective Inspector Rebus. I know you don't say much ...' he patted his jacket ... 'I've a notepad in my pocket if you need one.'
> [...] 'Can I ask you something, Major? Why

did you name your oilfield after an oatcake?
(p209)

Totally unused to such irreverent banter the Major
'reddened with sudden rage' (p209). Rebus, however, is
totally unfazed by the millionaire's anger.

As the plot unfolds, we learn that Rebus's lack of respect
for Major Weir is wholly justified. For Weir is not only
angling to dump a decommissioned oil platform in the
North Sea in a way that will be environmentally hazardous
but has also had an indirect hand in the death of Mitchison.
And to top it all, this same teetotaller, who will have an
employee sacked for even a whiff of alcohol on his breath,
happens to be guilty of the incestuous abuse of his own
daughter.

Rebus outspokenness, however, is not reserved for oil
moguls. He is equally good at speaking his mind to members
of his own police hierarchy. While investigating the connection of Tony El to Uncle Joe Toal, he visits Partick police
station and, noting the general air of prosperity amongst
his colleagues in the west, suspects corruption:

> Rebus thought of the fancy suits everyone
> seemed to be wearing, the good watches
> and shoes, the general air of prosperity and
> superiority.
> It was west coast dirt [...] (p76)

Later, meeting up with Chief Inspector Charles Ancram
in a Glasgow bar, Ancram offers him a drink. Rebus's reply
is pointed:

> 'Thanks, I will,' said Rebus, wishing he didn't
> feel so calm. 'Since you seem to be so loaded.
> Nice suit, too.'
> The humour left Ancram's eyes. 'There's a
> tailor on Argyle Street, ten per cent discount
> for serving officers. The eyes narrowed. 'Spit it
> out.'
> [...] 'Well, Rebus went on, 'everyone knows
> the west coast is open to bungs. Not always
> cash, you understand. Could be watches, ID

bracelets, rings, maybe even a few suits ...'
(p102)

Although Ancram is of use to Rebus in his Tony El
inquiries, Rebus does not curb his criticisms of what he sees
as corruption in Ancram's territory, even when he learns
Ancram is to be in charge of an internal inquiry which may
well see Rebus found guilty of wrongdoing in the Lewis
Geddes/Lenny Spaven case. He returns to the charge of
corruption, even when Ancram is trying to do a deal with
Rebus to drop his inquiry into the Mitchison affair lest it
jeopardise Ancram's own inquiry into Uncle Joe. For this,
he is prepared to produce a favourable report. Ancram
argues pragmatically:

> 'Wake up to reality. This isn't a linoleum
> floor, big squares of black and white.'
> 'No, it's grey silk suits and crisp green cash.'
> (p281)

Although he stands much to gain by going along with
Ancram's offer, Rebus here refuses to compromise and even
reiterates his charge of corruption against a superior officer,
feeling that this deal may benefit a major criminal as well
as Rebus himself. And Rebus's suspicions of corruption in
the Glasgow police may well be correct. For although
Rebus's work in Aberdeen helps Ancram track down one
crime syndicate, the general air of prosperity which Rebus
notes amongst Ancram and his colleagues is never properly
explained. A question mark lingers over possible criminal
infiltration of the Glasgow police.

Chief Inspector Edward Grogan of the Grampian Police
is yet another hierarchy superior to whom it would have
been pragmatic of Rebus to have shown some deference
since Grogan is holding him (at the instigation of the
corrupt cop Ludovic Lumsden) on suspicion of the murder
of Vanessa Holden, Johnny Bible's fourth victim. Instead,
at the moment when there is the possibility of Grogan
releasing him into the hands of Ancram to return to Edinburgh, Rebus risks his escape, confronts him and:

> [...] stopped with his face inches from Grogan's.

> 'Are you on the take, sir?' It was fun to
> watch the balloon fill with blood, highlighting
> burst veins and ageing lines. (p274)

Although it is Grogan's officers, Lumsden and Jenkins,
who are found to be wholly corrupted by the underworld,
Grogan's remarks at celebrations to mark the tracking
down of Johnny Bible do something to suggest that Rebus's
belligerent challenge to Grogan may be justified:

> Grogan was refilling a cup. There were at
> least a couple of crates of whisky, and three
> of bottled beer.
> 'Where do you get this stuff?' Rebus asked.
> Grogan smiled. 'Oh, you know.'
> 'Pubs? Clubs? Places you're owed a favour?'
> Grogan just winked. (p470)

While Kayleigh Burgess and Eamonn Breen of *The
Justice Programme* may not enjoy hierarchical superiority
to Rebus they represent the all-powerful media. Such is the
strength of media influence that it pushes Rebus's nervous
boss to open an internal inquiry into the Lenny Spaven
affair, much to Rebus's contempt:

> TV seems to be about the only thing brass
> are afraid of. Villains don't scare them, but
> ten minutes of negative coverage, dearie me,
> no. Can't have that. (p366)

When, however, we examine this all-powerful *Justice
Programme*, the people behind it and its rationale, there is
a hollowness and triviality at its heart:

> High ratings for the first series – attractive
> presenter Eamonn Breen scooping women
> viewers – so now a second series was on the
> blocks, and the Spaven case – severed head,
> accusations, and suicide of a media darling –
> was to be the showcase opener. (p40)

High ratings, a sexy presenter and gory titillation: they
all suggest that this particular investigation into an alleged
miscarriage of justice is more about armchair entertainment than a genuine concern for the truth. Equally shallow

is Kayleigh Burgess, Breen's assistant, who, at the very
instant Rebus learns of his friend Geddes's death, produces
a microphone and attempts to interview him, brazenly
ignoring his emotional distress. She later passes on to
Breen – who in turn passes it on to Ancram – Rebus's
passionate interest in the Johnny Bible affair, which helps
get him arrested – temporarily – as a suspect in that murder
inquiry. Burgess, Breen and others of the media hound
Rebus day and night, camping out on his doorstep in their
attempts to feed their public any fresh snippets of information on a story decades old. Far from trying to win
them over to his side, Rebus treats them with undisguised
contempt. Confronting Breen and other members of the
press as he returns home one night with his traditional fish
supper, Rebus startles them by appearing at long last to
wish to make a statement:

> 'Ladies and gentlemen of the press, I have a
> short statement I'd like to make.'
> [...] The noise died down. Rebus held his
> wrapped package aloft.
> 'On behalf of the chip-eaters of Scotland,
> I'd like to thank you for providing our nightly
> wrappings.'
> He was inside the door before they could
> think of anything to say. (p146)

Again, in his awkward situation, Rebus could hope to
gain from cultivating the media and having his side of
events heard sympathetically. Instead, he chooses to
antagonise them further.

While Rebus may be far from guiltless in this Spaven
affair, his is a genuine – and agonising – attempt to understand and to come to terms with what truly transpired;
theirs, if we can judge by the programme's rationale and
their behaviour, is a fairly shallow attempt to titillate the
public and boost ratings.

Time and time again, we see Rebus turning his face
resolutely against any deference to 'people who matter',
even at moments and in situations where their good opinion
might be of use to him. As events turn out, we see that he

is right to do so. For we see that, in their different
ways, Weir, Ancram, Grogan, Breen and Burgess are all
morally compromised. (In at least one case we might add
criminally compromised.)

In his fiercely independent stand against them, Rebus
steadfastly sets his face against any form of self-serving
hypocrisy – a charge of which *they* all appear to stand
guilty to a greater or lesser extent. To the public at large
they may be 'people who matter' but Rebus sees through
the hypocrisy of their situation: Weir lords it over T-Bird
Oil, yet is guilty of incestuous abuse of his daughter;
Ancram is a senior figure in a police force which Rebus
continues to see as being rather too prosperous for its own
good; Grogan seems unaware that two of his officers are in
the pocket of the underworld and is himself not averse to
accepting generous 'gifts'; for Breen and Burgess mis-
carriages of justice seem more a form of entertainment than
genuine opportunities to seek out truth.

Leading representatives as they are of Scotland's business,
police and media communities, they are all revealed to be
considerably less than worthy of the respect that their
powerful public positions might claim for them. Rebus is
correct to treat them with scant respect since they are
hardly worthy of any. Yet the end of the novel sees all of
them unscathed by any public sanction. John Rebus – and
the reader – are the only witnesses to their professional
and personal hypocrisies.

Rebus and personal engagement
Like Charles Dickens and Anthony Powell before him,
Rankin delights in peopling his pages with hosts of deftly,
but economically, realised characters. As Rebus pursues his
investigations in Edinburgh, Glasgow, Aberdeen and in
various outposts of the oil industry, he encounters countless
characters whose subsequent importance to the plot the
reader can never immediately gauge. Paradoxically, however, Rebus may interact easily with all of them but he
engages meaningfully with very few. For Rebus is essen-
tially a loner. In one of the two passages in *Black & Blue*
where a perspective other than Rebus's is introduced (the

other coming from Bible John), Jack Morton sees his friend
Rebus as spending:

> [...] more time living in his own head than in
> the company of others. Even the pub he
> chooses to haunt was one with fewer than
> usual distractions [...] And when group acti-
> vities were arranged – fishing trips, golf com-
> petitions, bus runs – Rebus never signed up
> [... He was] a loner even in company, his brain
> only fully engaged when working on a case.
> (p372)

We remember, too, his solitary night drives:

> Sometimes he drove all night, not just through
> Edinburgh: down to Leith and past the work-
> ing girls and hustlers, along the waterfront,
> South Queensferry sometimes, and then up on
> to the Forth Bridge, up the M90 through Fife,
> past Perth, all the way to Dundee, where he'd
> turn off and head back, usually tired by then,
> pulling off the road if necessary and sleeping
> in his car. (pp13–14)

The ghosts of past cases seem more real to him than
people like Maclay and Bain with whom he shares an office
in Craigmillar. He does not relate easily to others but when
his emotions *are* engaged, he is capable of acts of loyalty
and generosity.

We learn this early on when his young colleague, Brian
Holmes, requests his help in dealing with a suspect who
claims Holmes beat him up while in custody. Rebus is
resolutely uninterested in the truth of the claim but his
response is immediate, unquestioning and, we later learn,
effective. Holmes inquires:

> 'Aren't you going to ask me if I did it?'
> 'I don't *ever* want to know, understood? Who
> was the suspect?
> 'Mental Minto.'
> 'Christ, that brewhead knows more law than
> the procurator fiscal. OK, let's go talkies.'
> (p10)

Facing a caseload unusually complex, dangerous and time-consuming as he is, Rebus, nevertheless, involves himself closely throughout the novel in the fate of Holmes's marriage which is breaking up due to the pressures of trying to combine a police career with married life. Even at moments of personal crisis for himself, he takes time out to try to bring Brian and Nell together again.

To Gill Templer, one time 'significant other' in his life, he reveals a similar loyalty at moments when his own professional career is in crisis. She appeals to him over a tip-off she has had with regard to a major drug deal which is about to take place. Recently promoted to be one of the few female Chief Inspectors in Scotland, she is anxious not to fail in following it up. Rebus response to Gill is as supportive as it was to Brian:

> 'Someone's passed me some information about a drug deal ... a biggie.'
> 'Which protocol dictates you should pass on to the Scottish Crime Squad.'
> She gave him a look. 'And hand those lazy bastards the glory? Come on, John.'
> 'I've never been a great believer in protocol myself. All the same ...' All the same: he didn't want Gill fucking up. He could see this was important it was to her [...] (p114)

As we later find out, this drugs haul is connected with Rebus's inquiries at Burke's Club in Aberdeen. Rebus plays no small part in clearing up the affair but he is anxious throughout that it is Gill who gets the credit for solving this difficult and complex case.

> 'The thing is, Gill,' he said after another sip of wine, 'I think you were on to something big. And I think it can be salvaged. I just want to be sure it's *your* collar.'
> She looked at him. 'Why?'
> 'Because of all the Christmas presents I've never given you. Because you deserve it. Because it will be your *first*.'
> 'It doesn't count if you've done all the work.'
> 'It'll count all right [...]' (p345)

But if Rebus's generosity to a favourite young colleague and former 'significant other' is understandable, his kindness to Kayleigh Burgess is less easily explained. She, we remember, along with Eamonn Breen, has been making his life a misery with regard to *The Justice Programme* and had even inveigled herself into his flat with her recording machine (which Rebus had duly trashed). When she comes with a bottle of Macallan malt whisky as a peace offering, they share it and she falls asleep in Rebus's flat. Mellowed perhaps by the malt, Rebus's attitude to her is surprisingly benevolent, caring and, indeed, tender:

> He could wake her, help her into a taxi. He could drive her home, Glasgow under an hour away at this time of night. But instead he covered her with his duvet, left the music on so low he could barely hear Viv Stanshall's intros. He sat in his chair by the window, a coat covering. The gas fire was one, warming the room. He'd wait until she till she woke up in her own time. Then he'd offer a taxi or his services as a driver. Let her choose. (p152)

This generosity towards someone who is regularly the bane of his life stems from seeing in her a trait that they share: obsession with their respective jobs. Under the influence of the Macallan, he recognises in her someone who is as driven as he is by obsessive dedication to work, someone whose leisure hours are never spent far away from the job, or at least someone who can never feel totally at ease if they are.

> She needs a break, he thought, as in a rest. But she was obsessed with her job [...] It came down to guilt again, guilt and the work ethic. He thought of a story: World War One, Christmastime, the opposing sides emerging from their trenches to shake hands, play a game of football, then back into the trenches, picking up their guns again. (p151)

Rebus, we remember, is someone who is no stranger to obsession in this novel – his own with regard to the Bible

John/Johnny Bible case and that of Lewis Geddes in relation to Lenny Spaven. (Ian Rankin acknowledges that he thought at one point of calling the novel *Obsession*.) Indeed, the 'war' between Kayleigh and Rebus breaks out again before she leaves the flat, but this brief respite from hostilities reveals a quirkily gentle side to a man to whom acidic banter is a more usual response to those who upset him. Although this moment of gentleness is only passing, it helps illuminate a certain generosity in the interior life of this outwardly often abrasive man.

While Rebus's response to Kayleigh Burgess is more that of a father-figure than that of a sexually alert male, the same is far from being the case when he encounters Eve Cudden. Although Rebus does not know it at the time, their first meeting is no chance incident. Perched on a bar stool (classic position for the *femme fatale* in crime fiction) Eve has been set the task by Uncle Joe of finding out exactly what Rebus knows of the drugs/Burke's Club/Tony El connection. He pleads an early start as a reason for terminating their first meeting but there is no doubting his attraction to her:

> He felt her eyes were on him as he walked out of the bar towards reception. He had to force his feet up the stairs towards his room. Her pull was strong. (p189)

At this point we learn that

> Rebus had always found relationships with the opposite sex difficult. (p189)

Growing up in provincial Scotland where promiscuity was 'a bit behind the times' and later spending time in the army where women were either 'slags' or 'madonnas' (p190), Rebus's sexual relationships with women seem unsatisfactory, although 'women seemed to like him – that wasn't the problem' (p190).

Married and subsequently divorced, the call of his job 'had proved more seductive, more all-consuming than the relationship – than *any* relationship. (p190) Ever since his affairs had lasted 'months, weeks, mere days sometimes' (p190).

Nevertheless, the reaction described above to Eve reveals he is still capable of strong sexual attraction and eventually they will pass the night together (p404), with Eve indicating by her warm response to him that her interest in him is genuine and not entirely dictated by the fact that he turns a blind eye to her 'skimming' from Uncle Joe in return for helping put the murderous Malky away.

This fleeting moment of happiness, however, seems only to highlight the unsatisfactoriness of his sex life elsewhere. Rebus is a man ill at ease with his sexual self which he sees as being due not only to the demands of his job, but by his proximity to seeing women raped and killed. For as well as identifying with victims (as we have seen in an earlier section of this chapter), he sees a terrible and terrifying parallel between himself and the perpetrating criminals:

> The problem lay somewhere inside him, and it hadn't been eased by things like the Johnny Bible case, by women abused and then killed. Rape was all about power; killing, too, in its way. And wasn't power the ultimate male fantasy? And didn't he sometimes dream of it, too? (p190)

Standing back and looking at the multiple facets of his complex character, we see a man driven by many personal demons, some due to the painful empathy he shares with victims, others to the even more painful identification with victimisers, still others to the frustration he feels when he views the hypocrisy of public life around him. Reviewing all this, we cannot be surprised by the self-destructive but escapist preoccupation with drink, which we note increasing as the tempo of these particular cases increases until he arrives at the crisis described at the beginning of this section.

When Rebus and Morton have patched up matters, Jack, referring back to the fight, asks him:

> 'Is that why you drink? To stop this happen-ing?'

'Christ, Jack, I don't know. I drink because
I've always done it [...]'
'And you like to sleep without dreams?'
Rebus nodded. 'That most of all.' (p325)

Abrasive, uncompromising, bantering, Rebus is also, underneath his prickly, solitary, unkempt exterior, a gentler person than he would like strangers to think, a tortured human being who hears only too clearly, in Wordsworth's phrase, 'the still, sad music of humanity' which permeates his professional and personal life.

CHARACTERS

Detective Inspector Jack Morton

Although Jack Morton shares John Rebus's rank, that is almost all they share. Like certain other police officers in this novel, he appears as a foil to the character of Rebus. (The Oxford English Dictionary defines a foil as 'a person ... that contrasts with and so emphasizes the qualities of another.')

Jack Morton and Rebus go back a long way. Morton helped him solve the *Knots and Crosses* case at the beginning of the *Rebus* series of novels. Rebus meets up with him again in *Black & Blue* when he drives to Partick police station for his meeting with DCI Ancram. Rebus is astonished by Morton's appearance:

> Rebus looked Jack Morton up and down, couldn't believe what he saw. Last time they'd met, Jack had been a couple of stone over-weight, a heavy smoker with a cough that could crack patrol-car windscreens. Now he'd shed the excess weight, and the perennial ciggie was missing from his mouth. More, his hair was professionally groomed and he was dressed in an expensive-looking suit, polished black shoes, crisp shirt and tie.
>   'What happened to you?'
>   Morton smiled, patted his near-flat stomach. 'Just looked at myself one day and couldn't understand why the mirror didn't break. Got off booze and the cigs, joined a health club.'
> (p68)

Jack, although looking good now, is a self-confessed alcoholic. He has travelled the same road to self-destruction that Rebus is currently travelling and will help pull him away from alcohol and cigarettes. (This process culminates in a 'renunciation' scene in the Oxford Bar on pp352–3.)

Assigned to shadow Rebus's movements by Ancram until the trumped-up 'inquiry' into Rebus involvement in the Vanessa Holden murder is concluded, he uses the time to help Rebus face up to the self-destruction he is heading for unless he mends his ways.

Under Jack's influence, the bleak flat in Arden Street has its taste of proper cooking in many years and Morton encourages and assists Rebus in his redecorating of the flat.

As well as being a physical contrast to the unkempt and unfit Rebus, he also contrasts to him in his view of policing. Dragged down to Leith by Rebus on one of his pilgrimages to view Angie Riddell's 'pitch', he remonstrates with his friend for what he sees as his unhealthy preoccupation with the affair:

> 'John, we're not priests, you know. I mean, this is a *job*, right? You have to be able to lay it aside sometimes.'
>
> 'Is that what you do, Jack? Home after a shift, and suddenly everything's OK? Doesn't matter what you've seen out there, your home is your castle, eh?'
>
> Jack shrugged, hands rubbing the steering wheel. 'It's not my life, John.' (p294)

But policing *is* Rebus's life and he *does* see his job as a kind of vocation – as does a priest – rather than simply paid employment. Although a definite force for good in Rebus's life, Morton is seen by Rankin as lacking Rebus's depth of feeling and character. He is a happier, if shallower, person and policeman.

This fact is noted by no less a person than Bible John who has them both under surveillance at one point. Of Morton he remarks:

> A man Rebus's age, maybe a little younger, quite a tough-looking individual. Another policeman? Perhaps. The man's face lacked Rebus's intensity [...] Physically, Rebus's friend seemed the superior, but that wouldn't make Rebus a pushover. Physical strength could take a person so only so far.
>
> After that, it was down to attitude. (p362)

Perhaps the saddest thing about Jack Morton is that he

knows himself that nowadays he lacks this 'attitude' of
intensity that Bible John remarks on. He sees – to his own
disadvantage – the differences that now exist between him
and Rebus with whom he had once formed 'an effective
team' (p372):

> *He* might have changed – become a 'yes' man,
> a pencil-pusher, a careerist – but John was
> the same as always ... (p373)

A lesser man than Rebus in his commitment to policing,
it is, nevertheless, Jack Morton who sees Rebus through
the two severe personal crises in the book, one from
internal forces, the other from external ones.

The first is when Rebus's pent-up emotions finally ex-
plode on page 325 after talking to Mick Hine about Lenny
Spaven. His guilt and frustration seek release in physical
violence and Jack takes the brunt – quite literally – of this
cathartic lashing-out and helps him understand some of
the reasons for his destructive feelings. The second is when
Rebus acts impulsively – and totally against police
procedures – in going to meet up with Judd Fuller at
Burke's Club without telling anyone where he was going.
Jack works out what has happened and turns up in the nick
of time to help Rebus – in severe agony from torture by
Fuller – to escape.

Although a good friend and a decent man, Morton, with
his detached professionalism, contrasts sharply with Rebus
and his dedicated if self-destructive approach to policing.
He seems a more balanced yet somehow lesser human
being.

Detective Sergeant Ludovic Lumsden

Rebus first encounters him when he travels to Aberdeen to
ask questions about Allan Mitchison and his alleged killer,
Tony El. Lumsden chaperones Rebus around Aberdeen and
the Bannock oil platform. Like Morton, he is another foil to
the character of Rebus, but under his well-dressed appearance, is a very different character to both Morton and
Rebus.

> Lumsden wore a blue blazer with shiny brass
> buttons, grey trousers, black slip-on shoes.
> His short was an elegant blue and white
> stripe, his tie salmon-pink. The clothes made
> him look like the secretary of some exclusive
> club, but the face and body told another story.
> He was six feet two, wiry, with cropped fair
> hair emphasising a widow's peak. His eyes
> weren't so much red-rimmed as chlorinated,
> the irises a piercing blue. No wedding ring.
> He could have been anywhere between thirty
> and forty years old. (p166)

Underneath this dapper, sporting appearance, the very
opposite of Rebus's, Lumsden is the archetypical corrupt
cop, in cahoots with Joe Toal's drugs ring and Burke's Club
owners, Judd Fuller and Erik Stemmons.

Reading Lumsden correctly is one of the challenges
that Rankin sets Rebus and the reader alike. Is Lumsden a
smart cop-about-town who just might be a little too well-
connected to Italian restaurant owners, American nightclub
owners and local prostitutes? Or is he something more
sinister?

No sooner does he meet Rebus than he begins to sound
him out – somewhat ingratiatingly – on his attitude to
enjoying police favours, giving the impression that he is
sharing information with Rebus that he would not share
with all and sundry:

> Lumsden smiled again. 'Some fellow officers I
> wouldn't tell that to, but somehow I think
> we're on the same wavelength. Am I right?
> (p169)

To which Rebus's reply is a noncommittal 'You could
be' (p169).

Rebus and reader alike need to work hard to decipher
the real Lumsden under the smart clothes and affable
exterior.

Almost his very first words to Rebus are a lie, however.
He claims never to have heard of Anthony Ellis Kane yet
he, like Tony El as we later learn (p388), is on the payroll

of the Toals with Tony El running drugs to the club on a
daily basis and Lumsden protecting that channel from the
club to the oil platforms.

He is keen to persuade Rebus that the wild stories he
may have heard about night life in Aberdeen belong to the
past and that now Aberdeen is 'strictly corporate' (p182).

Rebus is increasingly on his guard, knowing now 'he
was being sold a line' (p183). He also notices:

> [...] the restaurant meal had been 'taken care
> of', and the bouncer on the door of the club
> had nodded them through, bypassing the cash
> desk. (p183)

This is in marked contrast to Rebus's behaviour in the
Indian restaurant frequented by Allan Mitchison where
Rebus pays in full and learns, incidentally, that the owner
had already told Aberdeen CID that Mitchison sometimes
arrived with a woman, a fact suppressed by the Aberdeen
police.

When Tony El is found dead, Lumsden is keen that it
should be put down to suicide, despite the clear evidence
that the death is due to the action of a Stanley knife, the
hallmark of a Malky Toal killing.

Rebus's provocative questioning of Erik Stemmons with
regard to the drug dealing he has noticed going on at
Burke's Club leads first to a warning – a pistol-whipping –
by Judd Fuller and later that same night to Rebus's arrest
for the alleged murder of Vanessa Holden, Johnny Bible's
fourth victim. This latter is a move engineered by Lumsden
to protect himself, Burke's Club and the Toals, who all
stand to lose if attention is drawn to their corrupt business
by Rebus's successful persistence in penetrating beneath
the clean image of Burke's that Lumsden is keen to peddle.

Lumsden's hypocritical pose as a good officer is wholly
convincing to his boss, Detective Chief Inspector Grogan,
who continually refuses to listen to Rebus's charges of
corruption against him. 'Justice' for Lumsden comes only
when Rebus informs Fuller that Lumsden has informed on
him to the Scottish Crime Squad which is launching an
operation. Lumsden is picked up by Fuller and tortured in

the same cellar as was Rebus. It is only due to Rebus's tipping off of his colleagues of his possible location that he is rescued, taken to hospital where an officer of the Crime Squad waits to take his statement. Rebus cannot resist some mild triumphalism to Grogan:

> '*That's* how clean Lumsden is. About time
> you woke up to the fact.' (p475)

Clean-cut, well-dressed, socially poised, well thought of by his superiors, Lumsden is on the surface and, indeed, in his inner self, everything that Rebus is not. His attractive appearance conceals an inner rottenness, for he is one of the key facilitators of the vice enveloping the North East's oil industry, a fact which it takes the unprepossessing and shabby Rebus to expose.

Chief Inspector Charles Ancram

Here is yet another police officer whose moral values serve to draw contrasts with those of Rebus. While Lumsden is finally seen as unquestionably allied with the criminal under-world of the North East, Glasgow-based 'Chick' Ancram remains a more enigmatic figure.

Ancram and Rebus enjoy a troubled relationship, despite Ancram twice proving useful to Rebus. Rebus first encounters him when researching into Tony El (chief suspect in the killing of Mitchison) and his employer, Uncle Joe Toal, a leading Glasgow gangster. Through Ancram, Rebus learns that Tony El may in fact be working in Aberdeen and not down south, as Toal would have him believe. Later, Ancram extricates Rebus from the thuggish DCI Grogan (admittedly for his own reasons) after his arrest as a suspect in the murder of Vanessa Holden.

His role elsewhere in the novel, however, is a vexatious one for Rebus. While meeting with Ancram in the west, Rebus notices what sees as the over-prosperous appearance of the officers in Ancram's division. He also notes from the files that Toal always seemed to be tipped off whenever investigation threatened and comes to the conclusion that:

> [...] someone in CID was feeding gen back to
> the gangster. Rebus thought of the fancy suits
> everyone seemed to be wearing, the good
> watches and the shoes, the general air of
> prosperity [...] (p76)

Putting two and two together Rebus deduces police
corruption and antagonises Ancram by saying as much.
This is a bad move on Rebus's part for Ancram is shortly
nominated to take charge of the internal inquiry into the
Spaven affair in which Rebus is now the only surviving
witness.

From this point onwards, a protracted game of cat-and-
mouse takes place as Rebus takes off for Aberdeen to avoid
Ancram's succession of answering-machine messages
demanding inquiry interviews.

Run to earth eventually in Aberdeen, Rebus is taken
back to Edinburgh by Ancram. While driving south, Rebus
and Ancram have a defining conversation in which their
values are explored. Ancram wants Rebus to drop his
investigation into the Mitchison affair since it is getting in
the way of his own projected surveillance on the Toal
empire, hinting that if he were to do so, it might do
Rebus 'a power of good' (p281) in the Spaven inquiry. Rebus
suspects Ancram's motives as being aimed at doing Uncle
Joe 'another good turn' (p281) Ancram pleads pragmatism
here, suggesting that 'people like Uncle Joe don't go away:
you get rid of them and a young pretender starts making
claims' (p281).

Ancram, puzzlingly, appears here to be both discussing
future action against the Toals and at the same time
condoning leaving existing criminals in place rather than
having to deal with newer versions of the same. Rebus
responds angrily, rejecting what he sees as a self-serving
compromise on Ancram's part leading to a delay which
might lead to further deaths.

Here there is clearly no meeting of minds. Rebus longs,
in Ancram's words, for 'black and white' values, whereby
criminals are caught and punished and victims avenged.
Ancram sees these values as being unrealistic in the real

world. Whether he does so from reasons of self-interest or from a pragmatic acceptance of the inevitability of one criminal filling the vacuum of another is never made quite clear.

How keen is he really to put Uncle Joe away?

Thanks to Malky's taped confession to Rebus, Ancram *will* have Uncle Joe, despite what he sees as Rebus messing up his projected surveillance. He seems, however, curiously ungrateful in a phone call to Rebus in the final pages and appears more irritated at having no hard evidence against the suspected mole in CID than satisfied at having Uncle Joe at long last in his sights:

> 'You've really mucked things up. If we'd gone ahead against Uncle Joe, we could have had the mole.'
>
> 'You'll have Uncle Joe instead.' Ancram grunted a response. 'You *know* who the mole is?'
>
> 'I have a hunch. Lennox, you met him that day in The Lobby [...] Thing is, I've no hard evidence.' (p492)

Rankin appears to wish to leave the matter of the relative rights and wrongs of both men's behaviour un-resolved. Rebus *may* have 'crossed the line' between correct and incorrect police behaviour in the Geddes/Spaven affair; Ancram, too, *may* have done the same thing in living so complacently with Uncle Joe. Both matters are left suspended for the reader's own judgement.

Although Rebus may long for the black and white values of clearly demarcated right and wrong, Rankin, his creator, prefers to suggest that the more muddied tones of *Black & Blue* in general – and Charles Ancram in particular – are really the ones which colour outcomes in criminal in-vestigation.

Bible John

Perhaps one of the boldest moves in an already ambitious novel was Rankin's introduction of the character of Bible John. With his arrival back in Scotland 'one fine Friday

morning' (p56), he leaves the world of fact (where he had
been responsible for three unsolved murders of women in
Glasgow in the 1960s) and enters the fictional world of
Rebus.

From the point of view of plotting, his is there to track
down Johnny Bible, a killer whose working methods are
very similar to his own in that he, too, has murdered three
women and taken away souvenirs from the victims. Far
from being flattered by the copy-cat killer, Bible John is
incensed and sets about tracking down the man he calls the
'Upstart'. In the use of this term we detect his con-
temptuous attitude to the person who appears to be
threatening his legend. When Johnny Bible increases his
tally to four murders, one more than Bible John, his mood
darkens even more:

> Four murders. One more already than Bible
> John of the sixties. It was galling, he had to
> say it. It rankled.
>   And someone would have to pay for it. Very
> soon. (p398)

More importantly, he is acutely aware that Johnny
Bible's re-awakening of media interest in his case threatens
his new identity as Ryan Slocum (p397) which is an even
stronger incentive to eliminate the Upstart.

Somewhat arrogantly, yet accurately, he believes that
he is well ahead of the authorities in the search for Johnny
Bible in that, as a serial killer himself, he had 'inside
knowledge of how a serial killer worked, thought and lived'
(p58). Although well ahead of the police forces of Edinburgh, Glasgow and Aberdeen, he had not counted on the
obsessive interest in the case of John Rebus. Rebus's name
turns up, as does that of a certain 'Peter Manuel' (the
name of a notorious hanged murderer which he suspects
the Upstart has borrowed) when Bible John checks out the
names of the handful of people who have consulted the 'Scotsman' and 'Glasgow Herald' files for the period of his own
murders. Were Rebus later to carry out similar checks, the
trail might lead back not only to the Upstart but, more
worryingly, to Bible John himself. The situation becomes

more acute when Bible John realises that he has given his business card to Rebus when they met – by an almost Dickensian coincidence – at an oil conference in Aberdeen. At that point Rebus becomes a potential target:

> The card might mean something to the policeman sometime down the road. Could Bible John risk that? He seemed to have two options: quicken his hunt for the Upstart.
>   Or take the policeman out of the game. (p193)

And so John Rebus, adding to his many other woes in the novel, now finds himself a potential target of one of Scotland's most infamous killers. Luckily for Rebus, the quest for Johnny Bible is long and complicated, and in the event, the only harm Rebus suffers from Bible John is that his flat is broken into when the latter attempts to retrieve that card.

But as well as meeting the needs of Rankin's plot, the presence of Bible John adds a telling commentary on the character of Rebus himself. With the exception of the comments of Rebus's long-time friend, Jack Morton, (p372) Bible John's observations comes closer than most to getting the measure of Rebus, underlining as they do the sterility of his life, his perceived loneliness and yet his singleness of purpose and sense of determination. (pp361–2)

Such insight may well stem from the fact that, although they find themselves of opposite sides of the law, law-officer and murderer, they have more in common than either would probably like to admit. (Not surprising, then, is the fact that when they are brought face to face for the only time in the novel (pp179–81) they hit it off quite well.) Nevertheless, they differ in one important way.

There is a yawning gulf in their attitudes to the value of human life. Rebus, as we know, carries with him the ghosts of every case he has worked on and demonstrates an empathy with 'all the victims he couldn't help and would never be able to help' (p325) to the point of feeling himself 'surrounded by loss.' With 'All the ghosts ... yelling at him ... begging him ... shrieking' (p381). For Bible John, however, victims appear to lack all humanity. He refers to the women Johnny Bible murdered as numbers: victims one, two, three and four. Rebus's 'Angie' is to Bible John just 'the Edinburgh prostitute'. And when he toys with the idea of killing Rebus he remarks:

> So many dead things around, what difference would another one make?
>   None at all. Not a jot. (p298)

To Bible John, a dead Rebus would just be one more of the 'many dead *things* around', not even a dead human being.

But allowing for this major difference in values, the parallels in their personalities are striking. For a start, both are loners. This we know from Morton's comments on Rebus and from our own observations of his solitary lifestyle. Slocum (to give Bible John the name he has adopted in his new life) is married, but Una Slocum seems to know little of her husband and the married life she describes seems sterile. In his job, too, he seems to distance himself from fellow employees by being away from his base for days on end (p398).

Both are driven by a private obsession: to track down Johnny Bible for their different reasons. (The piles of newspaper cuttings in Rebus's kitchen suggest that Bible John is *himself* yet another obsession of Rebus's.)

And just as Bible John carries around from home to home his chest full of souvenirs from his victims, so, too, does Rebus carry around, in Rankin's phrase, (*Rebus's Scotland, p20)* 'the ghosts of every victim'. They are men who, in their different ways, are reluctant to let go of the past.

Yet, paradoxically, in *Black & Blue* they are also refugees from the past: Rebus from his involvement in the Geddes/Spaven affair; Slocum from a past that he is reluctant to see raked up again through the activities of Johnny Bible. (We remember, too, how the Geddes/Spaven affair is yet another connection in their lives: Geddes's grudge against Spaven was that he was reluctant to give up details of Ray Sloane (Ryan Slocum's real name) whom

Geddes suspected of being Bible John back at the time of the Glasgow murders.)

Despite the nationwide police hunt to catch Johnny Bible, Rebus and Slocum are also the only two characters (joined latterly by Siobhan Clarke) who identify Johnny Bible. Indeed, the tension of the last pages of the novel stems from the reader wondering who will get to Johnny Bible first once they have both worked out the connection between the four victims, Johnny Bible and the oil industry.

In the event, Bible John triumphs. Leastways, he gets to Johnny Bible first and eliminates him. The price demanded, however, is the abandonment of his hard-won new identity and Bible John is forced to disappear once again. Both Slocum and Rebus are left at the end in rather similar positions. Like Rebus, Slocum has escaped the immediate threat from the past but neither, given the notoriety of one and the self-torturing doubts of the other, will ever, we suspect, be wholly free of its shadow.

It is perhaps fitting, therefore, that the last paragraphs of the novel are devoted to a strange telephone call which Rebus receives. There is a ghostly presence but no one at the other end speaks. Is this Bible John? Is the call a veiled threat to someone who has come closer to blowing his cover than anyone else before him? Or is it a reaching out to someone whom Bible John had never really thought of as an adversary? (p360). We remember, too, their parting words to each other in Aberdeen:

> 'Take care, Ryan.'
>   'You, too. It's a mad, bad world out there.'
> (p181)

Few would know better than Rebus or Bible John the truth of that latter statement. Is the phone call then a tacit acknowledgement of their shared, solitary status – in parallel universes – somewhere 'north of hell' (p493)?

Detective Sergeant Brian Holmes
The police officers we have encountered so far represent a contrasting diversity of policing values. Holmes is to be

viewed somewhat differently; he is a police officer who, for much of the novel, is still trying to work out what his values actually *are* and the effort is costing him dear.

> Holmes looked tired. Just a few years ago, he'd been young, fresh, keen. [...] Holmes's partner wanted him out of the force. She wanted someone who spent more time with her. Rebus knew all too well what she wanted. She wanted someone whose mind was on her when he was at home, who wasn't immersed in casework and speculation, mind games and promotion strategies [...] (p11)

Hence Holmes's dilemma: what does he value most? His life with his partner or his police career?

Torn between the two, Holmes allows the resulting frustration to drive him to behaving unprofessionally, to his clear distress. He has apparently beaten up a suspect who is now seeking retribution. Rebus intervenes in Holmes' favour, seeing much in Holmes that parallels his own early married life. Even at moments of crisis in his own investigations, he constantly checks up on the state of play between Holmes and Nell. He pleads with her to understand and accept Brian's dedication to his policing and tells her that leaving the force will be like 'a slow death' for him (p327).

Holmes himself, however, is finding it increasingly difficult to live with the strain of reconciling his police career with his marriage. Its toll is an undermining of his professional conduct. He confesses to having played by the rules and also to having overstepped the mark (as in the Mental Minto incident):

> 'I've tried both sides of the fence, hell, I've even tried sitting *on* the fence. No good, any of it.' (p493)

At one point (p318) Rebus draws parallels between the formative influence Geddes had on him and Rebus's own mentoring role on Holmes. The parallels are perhaps not entirely exact but are interesting nevertheless as Holmes clearly belongs in this trio of troubled policemen.

Like Geddes and Rebus before him, Holmes is a policeman who has behaved in a way that is open to question, to say the least. Like Geddes – but unlike Rebus, however – he subsequently puts personal life before career. (Geddes, we remember, chose to leave the police after his murky role in Bible John and Spaven affairs before retiring to Lanzarote with his beloved Etta.) Rebus, despite the many skeletons in his professional cupboard (referred to by Ancram on p102), has always chosen to soldier on, free of any close personal bonds.

This departure of Holmes, someone whom at one point Rebus absentmindedly refers to as 'son' (p. 237), casts a shadow over the final pages of the novel, leaving Rebus as it does an even more solitary figure in a police force where his close colleagues are few.

THEMES

The power of past sins

Throughout the novel a number characters are plagued by
transgressions committed decades earlier which return to
haunt their current lives. Dealing with the re-emergence of
these previous mistakes and crimes occupies three key
characters in the novel: Rebus himself, Bible John and
Major Weir.

In the case of Rebus the problem is occasioned by his
involvement with his old boss, Lawson Geddes. Twenty
years previously Geddes had been a much respected mentor
to the young Rebus. Geddes, however, had become obsessed
with bringing to justice a criminal called Lenny Spaven. In
the investigation into the murder of a woman called Elsie
Rhind, the name 'Lenny' emerged and a description by
friends tallied with the description of Spaven. Although no
other evidence existed to link Spaven to the crime, Geddes
was convinced of his guilt. One night he appeared at
Rebus's door and begged him to come with him to a lockup
where Geddes had seen Spaven enter. Rebus knew full well
there was a procedure to follow in these matters but so
strong was Geddes's obsession to nail Spaven that Rebus
allowed himself to go along with him. In searching the
lockup (without a search warrant) Geddes 'found' items
later identified as having belonged to Elsie Rhind.
Furthermore, they concocted a story of an anonymous tip-
off to explain their unauthorised search. Privately, Rebus
suspected the items may have been planted there by Geddes
on an earlier visit but does not speak out. Spaven was
found guilty on the basis of this evidence, sent to prison
(protesting his innocence loudly) and later committed
suicide. Geddes shortly afterwards resigned from the
police, subsequently moved to Lanzarote and in the course
of *Black & Blue* commits suicide following the death of his
wife.

Following Spaven's suicide, a TV channel has taken up
his cause. Now that Geddes is dead, Rebus alone is left to
face the music. The TV company's interest triggers an
internal police inquiry which Rebus spends much of the

novel avoiding. The threat to his career is a grave one if the internal inquiry decrees that the case be re-opened.

A suicide note from Geddes maintaining that the evidence had been genuinely found and not planted finally clears Rebus of guilt in the eyes of the law, but he remains severely tortured by his own doubts as to the truth of this statement from beyond the grave.

In Bible John's case, the offence from the past and the potential punishment he faces in the present are even graver.

Bible John was a real-life character who terrorised Glasgow in the late 1960s. As depicted in *Black & Blue*, Bible John had left Scotland after his third murder, accepting an offer of work in America. Rankin has him return several years prior to the events of this novel, however, and in this new existence he works as a respectable, married oil executive in Aberdeen. His quiet, anonymous life, however, is threatened by a series of copy-cat murders by someone nicknamed Johnny Bible by the press. He has caused the Bible John legend to resurface and with it the kind of media attention that Bible John is keen to avoid. Calling Johnny Bible contemptuously 'the Upstart', Bible John (or Ryan Slocum as he now is) sets out to eliminate him – and the unwanted media attention the Upstart has been attracting to what until now had been a fading legend.

His present existence is threatened by the ghost of his past life. He does in fact track down and eliminate the Upstart. But his realisation that the police could well be following the same trail as he did to find Johnny Bible (and therefore perhaps be closer to tracking *him* down), finally forces him to abandon that 'hard-fought-for-identity' (p397), his wife, career and home and disappear once again.

Major Weir, co-founder and president of T-Bird Oil, is yet another figure paying dearly for a crime committed years earlier. In the investigation of the murder of oil worker Allan Mitchison it emerges that his girlfriend, Joanna Bruce, is in fact the daughter of Major Weir. Bruce is a leading figure in the ecology movement which is vociferously and very publicly fighting a move by T-Bird Oil to decommission T-Bird Bannock oil platform in a way that would put the environment at risk. Bruce, we learn, had been abused as a child by Weir and had fled the family home many years earlier. Rather than involve the police, her revenge is to torment her father by her environmental protests. As Rebus comments to Jack Morton:

> 'He's in this little private hell she's constructed for the two of them. As long as he knows she's out there, demonstrating against everything he holds dear ... that's his punishment [...]' (p433)

In their very different ways, Rebus, Bible John and Major Weir have their present lives threatened by transgressions committed many years previously. While none of them is finally called to account by the law, that is not to say that they go unpunished.

In Rebus's case, while he is cleared of any wrongdoing by Geddes's suicide note, he himself is wracked by doubt as to the truth of this document as he confesses to Jack Morton:

> Jack patted Rebus's back. 'He's just cleared you, John. Wave this in Ancram's face and that's the end of that.'
>
> Rebus nodded, wishing he could feel relief, or any other sensible emotion.
>
> 'What's wrong?' Jack asked.
>
> Rebus tapped the paper. 'This is,' he said. 'I mean, most of it is probably right, but it's still a lie.'
>
> 'What?'
>
> Rebus looked at him. 'The stuff we found in the lockup I saw it in Elsie Rhind's house the first time we went round there. Lawson must have lifted it later.'
>
> Jack looked uncomprehending. 'Are you sure?'
>
> Rebus flew to his feet. 'No, I'm not sure, and that's the real bastard of it! I'll never be sure.' (p457)

We know from earlier confessions in the novel the extent to which Rebus suffers from guilt about crimes he has failed to solve. Living, then, with the suspicion that he may not only have allowed a real murderer to escape justice but to have been responsible for sending a man to prison unjustly, Rebus can hardly be said to have had his burden noticeably lightened by Geddes's letter, although, of course, the threat to his career is now a thing of the past.

Bible John, for his part, although smart enough to elude the police and imprisonment for his three murders, has had his 'hard-fought-for-identity' of nearly thirty years destroyed and is forced to walk away from everything he has achieved to date in his new life.

Major Weir, although legally still unpunished for his abuse, is regularly reminded of his guilt by his daughter's ecological protests 'against everything he holds dear'. Coupled with this is the threat of exposure and ruin hanging over his head should she choose to break her silence.

All three are forced, in their different ways, to come painfully to terms with the obstinate refusal of past sins to go away.

Fathers and children

Within the parameters of investigations into a number of murders, *Black & Blue* also explores a theme which recurs in other Rankin novels (*Let It Bleed, A Question of Blood*) – the idea of children posing various threats to their respective fathers for a number of different reasons.

'Uncle Joe' Toal, Glasgow's underworld boss, although making only one short appearance in the novel, is a significant figure. He controls moneylending, protection, prostitution and betting in Glasgow and is currently engaged in expanding his criminal empire by peddling drugs into oil-rich Aberdeen. This activity is gradually found to be the motor for many turns in the plot. For this expansion of his empire he employs his only son, Malky, nicknamed 'Stanley', from his relish for killing people with a Stanley knife. It is his murder of Tony El (responsible earlier for the death of Allan Richardson which opens the story) which first draws him seriously to Rebus's attention.

The psychopathic Malky is working against his father

in two ways. He is deeply in love with his father's live-in mistress, Eve Cudden, and the pair of them have been sleeping together. But he not only threatens his father's domestic arrangements; he is undermining his father's illicit operations in Aberdeen as well by skimming money from Toal's operations in order to run away with Eve (although she has other ideas.). Such is Malky's growing eminence in the underworld that Rebus speculates that Malky (and Eve) may even ultimately be planning to oust his father entirely:

> Maybe they think they're stronger than him.
> Maybe they reckon in a war the muscle-men
> would change sides. Stanley's the one people
> are scared of these days [...] (p369)

The idea of offspring working against the father is taken up again in the episodes involving Major Weir and his daughter, Joanna Bruce. Here, too, we have a child threatening the business empire of a parent but for very different reasons. Here the reason is not personal ambition but personal revenge. The victim of abuse by her father, Joanna Bruce takes up the cause of ecological protest against oil industry practices, knowing that her action is the most painful form of vengeance she can exact for the violation she has suffered at her father's hands. The threat grows more ominous still when Allan Mitchison, Bruce's boyfriend and fellow victim of abuse as a child, attempts to blackmail Weir, an action which could have led to his public disgrace which, interestingly, Bruce herself does not seek. Hers is a much subtler form of punishment – 'demonstrating against everything he holds most dear'. (p. 433) This is a crueller and more long-lasting torment than any prison sentence that a court of law could hand out.

Bible John, too, suffers a threat to his wellbeing from his offspring. The offspring this time is not of the biological but rather the spiritual kind, for that is how Johnny Bible is referred to several times by the media:

> [...] Bible John, supposing he were still alive,
> would be in his mid-to-late fifties, while
> this new killer was described as mid-to-late

> twenties. Therefore: Johnny Bible, spiritual
> son of Bible John. (p8)

We learn towards the end of the novel that Johnny Bible
had clearly carried out his murders as an act of homage to
his spiritual father, turning a room in his house into 'a
shrine to Bible John' (p468). Here the threat to the 'father'
is not posed out of ambition or revenge but out of
admiration. This is admiration that Bible John could well
have done without, threatening as it does the identity he
has spent three decades honing and, consequently, his
freedom. This homage is ill-viewed by Bible John and poses
an awkward problem:

> He'd considered the dilemma over long days
> and nights – on one side of the scales, his wish
> to track down the Upstart; on the other, the
> risk that in so doing, he would be putting
> himself – his identity – in danger. (p59)

His hope is that 'he'd get to Johnny Bible before the
police did.' (p58) In this he is successful but, knowing
the police are following in his own tracks, he is forced to
abandon his present life and disappears into the unknown.
Discussing Bible John, or rather Ryan Slocum as he is now
called, with Rebus, Una Slocum comments on their child-
lessness with unwitting irony:

> I think Ryan would have liked a son. (p483)

As it happened, he did acquire one – but 'fatherhood'
gave him no pleasure, causing nothing less than the de-
struction of a life carefully constructed over thirty years

Intriguingly, this theme running through the text lightly
touches Rebus's life also. Talking about Rebus's daughter
Sammy – who does not appear in this novel – Jack Morton
enquires at one point if she went to university. Rebus
replies that after secretarial college she works for SWEEP,
a charity dealing with the needs of prisoners leaving jail.

Morton comments:

> 'Working with ex-cons?'
> 'That's it.'
> 'Did she do it to have a dig at you?'

> Rebus had asked himself the same question
> many times. He shrugged.
>   'Fathers and daughters, eh?' (p327)

The various actions which Malky Toal, Joanna Bruce
and Johnny Bible set in motion – whatever their personal
motives for them – end disastrously for all three. Malky
Toal, tricked by Rebus into a confession of the killing of
Tony El, finds himself locked up for his murder, an event
which allows his unwilling 'lover', Eve, to abscond with the
proceeds of their skimming from his father. Johnny Bible's
copy-cat murders, although a warped kind of homage to
his spiritual father, result in his death at the hands of
Bible John. Joanna Bruce's environmental–protest activities
against her father lead indirectly to the death of the only
person she has ever appeared to care for, Allan Mitchison.

As for the people on the receiving end of these un-
welcome attentions, they, too, pay a heavy price. Rebus
appears to think (p. 492) that Ancram can at long last move
against the criminal empire of Uncle Joe, thanks to Malky's
confession. Bible John loses his new identity and is forced
to flee once he has killed Johnny Bible, while Major Weir
lives with the threat of exposure hanging over him and the
daily reminder of his abuse in the shape of the relentless
protests of his daughter against T-Bird Oil.

The effects of the oil industry

In *Black & Blue*, Rebus explores the oil industry, or more
precisely, the people it attracts and its pervasive and
corrosive effects. It is the common factor linking all the
deaths in the plot.

Rankin, however, attempts to be objective in presenting
the industry. Balancing the early euphoric myths with the
later backlash, he seeks the middle ground. Rebus calls to
mind the birth of the industry in the north-east:

> Rebus recalled the early oil years, the sound
> of Lowlanders scurrying north looking for
> hard work at high wages [...] It was Scotland's
> Eldorado [...] There were jobs going spare, a
> mini-Dallas was being constructed from the

> husk of a fishing port. It was unbelievable, incredible. It was magic. (p163)

But soon, however:

> [...] the initial stories of Eldorado turned into tales of the dark side: brothels, blood-baths, drunken brawls. Corruption was everywhere [...] (p164)

Reviewing all this, Rebus comments:

> And somewhere in the middle, between Hell and Eldorado, sat something approximately the truth, nothing like as interesting as the myths. Economically the north-east had profited from oil, and relatively painlessly at that. (p164)

Indeed, superficially, the world of oil is represented well, attractively even, and peopled by decent folk for the most part. Heading for the T-Bird Oil Headquarters Rebus notes the surroundings positively enough:

> The area around the airport was a mix of farming land, new hotels, and industrial complexes. T-Bird Oil had its headquarters in a modest three-storey hexagon, most of it smoked glass. There was a car park at the front, and landscaped gardens with a path meandering through them to the building itself. (p171)

Inside, he meets Stuart Minchell, T-Bird's Human Resources manager and Rebus's contact with regard to the death of Allan Mitchison. Minchell is polite, helpful, a member of Greenpeace and a contributor to Oxfam. Through Minchell's help Rebus arrives at the Sullom Voe refinery on Shetland and allows himself to be impressed:

> Sullom Voe was huge. It had taken seven years to build, breaking all sorts of records in the process [...] and Rebus had to admit it was an impressive monster. [...] And if you looked out past the crude oil tanks and the unloading jetties, you saw water – the Voe itself to the south; then Gluss Isle over to the west, doing a good impression of unspoilt

> wilderness. It was like a sci-fi city transported
> to prehistory.
>   For all of which, the process control room
> was about as peaceful a place as Rebus had
> ever been [...] (pp214–15)

The quiet helpfulness of the personnel Rebus meets here
is matched by that of the thoroughly decent Willy Ford,
Allan Mitchison's room-mate on the Bannock oil platform.
A man of equal integrity is Jake Harley, seemingly Allan
Mitchison's only other friend, who is also employed by T-
Bird Oil and deeply concerned with the ecological future of
his country.

All this presents a positive view of the oil industry, its
achievements and personnel; but behind it there lies
another less positive reality which is only gradually
exposed as Rebus pursues his enquiries into the death of
Allan Mitchison.

One character calls the world of the oil platforms 'a real
frontier' (p169), existing as it does on the line between the
norms of society and a world living by its own laws, rather
reminiscent of the old Wild West. Throughout the novel
Rebus is obliged to explore both sides of this frontier which
separates the twin realities of the oil industry – the
legitimate force for economic prosperity and the more law-
less, money-driven corrupter of morality. The problem, as
he finds out, is determining where exactly the frontier lies
and who belongs on which side of it.

From an investigation into the death of a humble painter
in a Niddrie slum, Rebus's enquiries expand ever outwards
until they lead him to a full understanding of a net of vice
that covers Scotland, one spun largely by the rich returns
from the oil industry.

How then does the oil industry link the characters and
influence the action of *Black & Blue*?

The Mitchison Death. Allan Mitchison, whose death
triggers Rebus's interest in the case, has been employed as
a painter at Sullom Voe and on the Bannock oil platform
in the North Sea. While at Sullom Voe he made the

acquaintance of Jake Harley, a committed environmental-ist, who mentioned to him an oil spill at Sullom Voe from the tanker *Negrita*. He in turn talked of it to his girlfriend, Joanna Bruce, the estranged daughter of T-Bird Oil chief, Major Weir and committed environmentalist. In tracing the confused ownership of the *Negrita*, Bruce discovers that the real owner of the tanker is T-Bird Oil. This discovery is made at a sensitive time for the company since the Bannock oil platform is coming to the end of its natural life and T-Bird Oil is trying to convince the government that their solution of sinking the platform rather than dismantling it expensively is the best option. News of their incompetence over the *Negrita* could well destabilise this. Such in-formation would have given the green lobby powerful ammunition against T-Bird Oil, who are opposing the ecologically harmful solution preferred by Weir and his accountants. Mitchison oversteps the mark, however, by trying to strengthen their case by attempting to blackmail Major Weir with the fact of his incest with his daughter. Weir asks his PR guru Hayden Fletcher to deal with the matter who employs Tony El. This latter's intervention leads to the death of Mitchison. His death is a direct result of his unwise attempts to influence the decommissioning of an oil platform.

The Johnny Bible Murders. When Rebus begins his investigation into Mitchison's death, these murders are already engaging the police forces of Edinburgh, Glasgow and Aberdeen, the cities in which the serial killer has struck. Despite their best efforts, their enquiries are leading nowhere. It is only Rebus and Bible John who begin to see a pattern in the killings. They are the only ones to notice that the first three victims (and a later fourth) all have a connection (although not always an obvious one) with either the oil industry itself or with people who are themselves connected with oil. Bible John, who, under his new identity of Ryan Slocum is himself employed in an oil-related industry, is the first to make the connection. He takes it upon himself to eliminate Martin Davidson (alias Johnny Bible) who, it turns out, is also employed in an oil-related service industry. It is Johnny Bible's oil industry related activities which allow him the freedom to travel throughout Scotland pursuing his murderous intentions.

The Burke's Club Connection. Burke's Club is the face of the oil industry at play and, as Rebus discovers in the course of his enquiries, a clearing-house for drugs, prostitution and pornography.

Founded by two Americans, Erik Stemmons and Judd Fuller, who had come to Aberdeen twenty years previously in the wake of the new oil wealth, Burke's Club is also a crossroads for many of the novel's intertwining strands.

Burke's Club is the place where Johnny Bible met his first victim, Michelle Strachan.

Burke's Club's phone number is found on the desk of Fergus McLure, a petty criminal inveigled into fronting the transport of drugs to Burke's Club but who, through fear, alerts the police and is promptly killed by Judd Fuller, as we later learn.

Burke's Club is also the hangout of Hayden Fletcher where he met Tony El and employed him to take care of the nuisance that Allan Mitchison was causing.

Burke's Cub is buying drugs from Uncle Joe Toal through his intermediaries, Eve Cudden, his son, Malky, assisted on a day-to-day basis by Tony El.

Burke's Club has the police officers with responsibility for oil industry liaison, Jenkins and Lumsden, on its payroll so that its owners can supply the rigs with drugs and pornography, untroubled by police investigations.

The wealth of oil industry employees funds Burke's Club and Burke's Club supplies them with all their illicit needs. Rebus sums up the symbiotic relationship between Burke's Club and the oil industry thus:

> The legit and the illicit working side by side,
> each feeding the other. (p391)

STRUCTURE AND STYLE

The novel's structure falls into six sections entitled *Empty Capital, The Whispering Rain, Furry Boot Town, Dead Crude, The Panic of Dreams* and *North of Hell*. The first four follow Rebus as he moves from Edinburgh, to Glasgow, then to Aberdeen (and Shetland) and finally to the Bannockburn oil platform. While each of the four charts a point in his geographic progress across Scotland, their titles sometimes hint as much about Rebus's current state of mind and situation as they tell us about the locations themselves.

In *Empty Capital* Rebus and Mitchison are seen to be sharing a current emptiness in their Edinburgh existences; in *The Whispering Rain* suspicions of police corruption suggest themselves to Rebus soon after he arrives in the rain-soaked west. ('Raintown', the name by which Rebus refers to Glasgow on page 67, is the name of an album by the Scottish band, Deacon Blue); *Furry Boot Town* is a word-play joke on the Aberdeen dialect; *Dead Crude* is a reference to the crude oil (which comes in dead and live forms) of the Bannock platform (and also perhaps to the crudity with which Rebus is framed as a suspect in the Johnny Bible case.) *The Panic of Dreams* reflects the turmoil in Rebus's mental state as the stresses in his personal and professional lives crowd together; and in *North of Hell* we see Rebus (who had begun in the 'purgatory' of Craigmillar) restored, if not exactly to happiness, to something less than the hell his life descended to at some points in the plot.

With the exception of brief observations by Bible John on Johnny Bible and Rebus and the commentary on Rebus's solitary lifestyle by Jack Morton, the action of the novel is seen through Rebus's eyes. Rankin has been careful to match the resulting narrative and dialogue to that which we would expect from the sharp-eyed, sharp-tongued Rebus. The writing style is spare and unadorned. Metaphors and similes are fairly rare. Sentences are often short, unencumbered with unnecessary adjectives or adverbs, sometimes omitting even verbs, conversational in tone:

Rebus tried the radio – vacuous pop, pounding
disco, telephone chat. Then jazz. Jazz was
OK. Jazz was fine, even on Radio Two. He
parked near Burke's, watched a dumb-show as
two bouncers took on three farm-boys whose
girlfriends were trying to pull them away.
'Listen to the ladies,' Rebus muttered.
'You've proved yourselves for the night.'
The fight dissolved into pointed fingers and
swearing, the bouncers, arms not touching
their sides, waddling back inside. A final kick
at the doors, saliva hitting the porthole-styled
windows, then hauled away and up the road.
Opening curtains on another north-east
weekend. Rebus got out and locked the car,
breathed the city air. Shouts and sirens up on
Union Street. He crossed the road and headed
for Burke's. (pp436–7)

In this brief passage Rankin is steering Rebus to his
fateful appointment at Burke's Club with Judd Fuller, but
at the same time manages to cram in information about
Rebus's opinion of Radio Two, the tripartite friction
between three stubborn farm-boys, their girlfriends and two
bouncers, a sly dig at muscle-bound body-builders and the
general tension in the Aberdeen night. With a film-maker's
eye for detail he sketches in only the essential to capture a
vibrant picture of Rebus's world at one particular moment
in time. While there is no attempt to fill in the overall
physical geography of the location, this moment in time is
brought vibrantly alive for us, thanks to a style which
maximises atmosphere from minimalist description. Em-
bedded in this cameo sketch, too, is the – as yet undetected
– threat from the waddling bouncers whose victim Rebus is
about to become. Readers cannot take any short cuts
through descriptions such as these, for while some details
are there simply to create the ambience of the moment,
certain others are there – as above – to hint at an
importance which will only later become clear. Rankin
introduces his characters in much the same way, in that
some carefully detailed minor figures (such as 'Heavy'
Maclay at the Craigmillar police station) are just that,

others (such as the anonymous 'braid-hair' protester outside
T-Bird Oil) assume a later importance not suspected at the
moment of their introduction.

Economy of style of a different kind is apparent when
Rebus is interviewed for a second time by Ancram as part
of the internal inquiry. Rebus cannot concentrate on
Ancram's methodical questioning as his own mind is racing
through the accumulating evidence. With a series of often
grammatically unconnected phrases, not only is Rankin
inviting us to be present in the frenzied turmoil of Rebus's
mind, but he is also using these broken, hectic utterances
to run through the various connections in the plotlines of
which we, as readers of this complex narrative, may well
need reminding:

> 'You didn't actually hear the conversation?'
> 'No.' Braid-hair and Mitchison ... Mitch the
> organiser, protester. Mitch the oil worker.
> Killed by Tony El, henchman to Uncle Joe.
> Eve and Stanley, working Aberdeen, sharing a
> room ...
> 'But DI Geddes told you it was to do with
> Mr Spaven? A tip-off?'
> 'Yes.' Burke's Club, police hang-out, maybe
> an oil workers' hang-out too. Hayden Fletcher
> drinking there. Ludovic Lumsden drinking
> there. Michelle meets Johnny Bible there ...
> (p365)

Here we see Rankin's style successfully inviting us
directly *into* Rebus's situation and thought processes.
Sometimes, however, Rankin chooses to *externalise* these, as
when Rankin has Rebus play music which in some way
sums up his current situation or state of mind. Sidelined
from normal investigative duties, for example, Rebus sets
about painting his flat with the help of Jack Morton:

> With his blue boilersuit on, Jack looked the
> part. Rebus handed him the roller, then
> reached under the sheet to put the hi-fi on.
> Stones, *Exile on Main Street*. Just right. The
> two of them got to work. (p315)

Such musical references at key moments are lyrical confirmations of the mood and situation currently being described in the narrative.

(Other types of references – literary and historical – turn up from time to time in *Black & Blue*, reminding us of Rankin's early career as a PhD research student: Rebus introduces Geddes' deathbed testimony to Ancram by referring to the title of two novels by Graham Greene, saying that Geddes' evidence is not so much 'the end of the affair' as 'the heart of the matter'; Allan Mitchison's effects include a copy of *Whit*, a novel by Rankin's fellow Fifer and contemporary, Iain Banks; a Major Weir was executed in Edinburgh in 1670 for, among other crimes, incest. Weir until his confession had been thought to be a blameless, pious pillar of the community ...)

A hallmark of Rebus's speech is his bantering style of interfacing with the world. Invited to a critical meeting with the Assistant Chief Constable, he asks the secretary:

> 'Will there be tea and biccies? I'm not coming otherwise.'

Coming across Major Weir reading the *Financial Times*, Rebus asks:

> 'Any chance of a keek at the racing results?'

Far from showing deference to authority in these situations, Rebus seems to revel in debunking them with his use of slangy diminutives and Scots vernacular.

Wisecracking word play also features in Rebus's dialogues. Thanked by Rebus for providing information, Minchell replies:

> 'My pleasure, Inspector, But next time you want a favour, try not to make it on a day when I'm due to sack a dozen of our work-force.'
> 'Hard times, Mr Minchell?'
> 'A book by Dickens, Inspector Rebus. Good-bye.'
> Jack was laughing. 'Good line,' he said approvingly.

'So it should be,' Rebus said, 'he was less
than half a mile away.' (p412)

In the context of a complex, multilayered narrative, it is
not difficult to see why Rankin cultivates this economic
deftness of style, eliminating all but the essential to convey
situations, states of mind and personalities. The intense
concentration required by the reader to follow the
convolutions of the various plots outlaws any style that
slows down the action or attempts to distract the reader
with an elaborately wordy prose style. And yet there is a
wealth of detail in his world. We feel we know well even
minor characters such as Ancram's 'snitch' or Feardie
Fergie – whom we never meet alive – thanks to a few well-
selected brushstrokes. Spare and lean, Rankin's style
nevertheless provides readers with the kind rich reading
experience which lingers in the mind long after the novel is
closed.

BIBLIOGRAPHY

Non-fiction:

Rebus's Scotland: Orion, London, 2005.

Writing as Ian Rankin: the Rebus Series:

Knots and Crosses: The Bodley Head, London, 1987.
Hide and Seek: Barrie & Jenkins, London, 1990.
Wolfman: Century, London, 1992 (Reissued as *Tooth and Nail*, Orion, London, 1998).
Strip Jack: Orion, London, 1992.
The Black Book: Orion, London, 1993.
Mortal Causes: Orion, London, 1994.
Let It Bleed: Orion, London, 1995.
Black & Blue: Orion, London, 1997.
The Hanging Garden: Orion, London, 1998.
Death Is Not the End: Orion, London, 1998 (Novella).
Dead Souls: Orion, London, 1999.

Set In Darkness: Orion, London, 2000:

The Falls: Orion, London, 2001.
Resurrection Men: Orion, London, 2002.
A Question of Blood: Orion, London, 2003.
Fleshmarket Close: Orion, London, 2004.
The Naming of the Dead: Orion, London 2006.
Exit Music: Orion, London 2007.

Writing as Ian Rankin:

The Flood: Polygon, Edinburgh, 1986.
Watchman: The Bodley Head, London, 1988.
Westwind: Barrie and Jenkins, London, 1990.

Writing as Jack Harvey:

Witch Hunt: Headline, London, 1993.
Bleeding Hearts: Headline, 1994.
Blood Hunt: Headline, 1995.

Short Stories:

A Good Hanging and Other Stories: Century, London, 1992.
Herbert in Motion and Other Stories, Revolver, London, 1997.
Beggars Banquet: Orion, London, 2002.

Criticism:

Plain, Gill: *Ian Rankin's 'Black & Blue'*: London: Continuum, 2002.

Useful Websites:

www.ianrankin.net
www.homespun.co.nz/exile/black.html (lists music and artists referred to throughout)
www. januarymagazine.com/profiles/ianrankin.html (rich in background detail)
www.orionbooks.co.uk/5814-1/Author-Ian-Rankin (useful source of interviews and reviews)